AMERICAN MUSEUM
OF NATURAL HISTORY

STERLING CHILDREN'S BOOKS
New York

An Imprint of Sterling Publishing Co., Inc.
1166 Avenue of the Americas
New York, NY 10036

ISBN 978-1-4549-2740-2

Distributed in Canada by Sterling Publishing
c/o Canadian Manda Group, 664 Annette Street
Toronto, Ontario, Canada M6S 2C8
Distributed in the United Kingdom by GMC Distribution Services
Castle Place, 166 High Street, Lewes, East Sussex, England BN7 1XU
Distributed in Australia by NewSouth Books, 45 Beach Street, Coogee, NSW 2034, Australia

For information about custom editions, special sales, and premium and corporate purchases, please
contact Sterling Special Sales at 800-805-5489 or specialsales@sterlingpublishing.com.

Manufactured in China

Lot #:
2 4 6 8 10 9 7 5 3 1
12/17

sterlingpublishing.com

Text written by Ben Richmond

IMAGE CREDITS
Alamy: © age footstock: 28; © blickwinkel: 11; © Danita Delimont: 28;
© Design Pics Inc.: 16 right; © John Lander: 21; © Craig Lovell/Eagle Visions Photography: 19 top;
© Natural Visions: 22 bottom, 30; © Papilio: 22 top; © Cheryl Schneider: 18;
© Keren Su/China Span: 9, 17, 23 top
Ardea: © Tom & Pat Leeson: back cover
Getty Images: © China Photos: 7
Minden Pictures: © Ingo Arndt: 27 top; © Eric Baccega: 1, 10,12;
© Bill Coster: 26; © Katherine Feng: 8, 15 top, 19 bottom, 23 bottom; © Mituaki Iwago: 20;
© Klein and Hubert: 5, 16 left, cover; © Cyril Ruoso: 27 bottom; © ZSSD: 2
Shutterstock: © Hung Chung Chih: 15 bottom; © Foreverhappy: 14, 24;
© Eric Isselee: back cover; © shejian: 13

American Museum of Natural History

Baby Panda Chews Bamboo

STERLING CHILDREN'S BOOKS
New York

In the mountains of central China, a baby panda is born. Baby pandas are called cubs. Panda cubs are born blind and do not yet have their signature black-and-white fur.

Tiny and helpless, the cub relies entirely on his mother to survive.

The cub sleeps in a den for a long time, cradled against his mother's chest. In those first few days, the mother does not leave the den—not even for a drink of water. She is focused on caring for her cub.

The cub drinks his mother's milk up to twelve times a day.

After a week, his fur begins to thicken.

After three months, the cub's fur has filled in, and he looks like
a tiny version of his mother.

He begins to crawl and finally roams beyond the den.

The world is huge—there is so much to see!

The mother begins teaching her cub valuable skills. She shows him good hiding spots. Together, they sit at the bottom of trees and under large stumps—but they are not simply lounging.

They are on the lookout for potential danger. Other animals that live in the mountains, like wild dogs or brown bears, may be looking for an easy meal, like a wandering panda cub.

The cub loves to play! Playing is important
because it helps the cub develop skills and
become stronger. He rolls around in the grass,
full of energy.

Later, he tries to climb a tree. Pandas are great climbers and also excellent swimmers.

The more the cub plays, the better he will become at these activities.

During all this time, the cub has been living off his mother's milk. At six months, the cub's molars have grown in. Molars are the big teeth that are the farthest back in your mouth. The cub is finally ready to take his first bite of bamboo.

CHOMP!

The cub can now eat chewy bamboo, but he also continues to drink his mother's milk. The milk is full of the nutrients and fat that he needs to grow to a healthy weight.

Pandas' molars are large and flat. They need these teeth to chew through the tough bamboo.

Pandas also have a bone on their front paw that works like a thumb and helps them hold the bamboo while they eat.

Pandas are very picky eaters. Ninety-nine percent of their diet is made up of bamboo. But sometimes they may eat bugs, rodents, and vines.

An adult panda spends nearly 14 hours a day eating. At the end of the day, he will have eaten about 25 pounds of bamboo!

Winter comes, but pandas don't hibernate—or sleep through the season—like some grizzly and black bears do. As the weather gets colder, the mother and her cub head down the mountain where it is warmer.

There, they continue eating and lounging as usual. When they are tired, they plop down in the snow and fall asleep.

Pandas sleep for two to four hours at a time, usually between meals. Their thick fur keeps them bundled and warm.

At one year old, the panda cub weighs about 80 pounds and no longer drinks his mother's milk. He is now considered a young panda. Though much larger than he was a year ago, the young panda still has some growing to do. In two years, he will weigh 200 pounds or more!

The young panda climbs up a tree and lies in the branches.

A few months pass before the young panda is fully independent. He can take care of himself and does not need his mother anymore. Pandas are solitary animals, meaning that they prefer to be alone. They use their sense of smell to detect if there are other pandas nearby.

When the young panda smells another panda in his area, he moves to a different part of the forest.

For a long time, pandas were endangered, which meant there weren't very many of them left in the world. The main problem was that the bamboo forests where pandas live were being cut down.

But today, things are different. The number of pandas in the world is now rising! Pandas are not endangered anymore, thanks to the people who work to protect these animals and their homes.

Meet the Expert

My name is **Angelo Soto-Centeno**, and I am a Research Associate in the Department of Mammalogy at the American Museum of Natural History. I have worked with different kinds of mammals such as pocket gophers, mice, and deer, but my specialty is bats. For my research, I study the reasons why some mammals have become extinct to understand how we can better preserve the ones that are alive today. The conservation of mammals such as pandas is important to maintain healthy ecosystems everywhere. Did you know that an average newborn panda is 1/900th the size of its mother?